Primary Social Studies for Antigua and Barbuda

WORKBOOK
GRADE 3

Anthea S Thomas

Published by Collins
An imprint of HarperCollins*Publishers*
The News Building
1 London Bridge Street
London SE1 9GF

HarperCollins*Publishers*
Macken House,
39/40 Mayor Street Upper,
Dublin 1,
D01 C9W8
Ireland

Browse the complete Collins catalogue at
www.collins.co.uk

British Library Cataloguing-in-Publication Data
A catalogue record for this publication is available from the British Library.

Author: Anthea S. Thomas
Commissioning editor: Elaine Higgleton
Development editor: Bruce Nicholson
In-house editors: Caroline Green, Alexandra Wells, Holly Woolnough
Copy Editor: Sue Chapple
Proof reader: Jan Schubert
Answer checker: Hugh Hillyard-Parker
Cover designers: Kevin Robbins and Gordon MacGilp
Cover image: Wectors/Shutterstock
Typesetter: QBS
Illustrators: QBS and Ann Paganuzzi
Production controller: Sarah Burke
Printed and Bound in the UK by Ashford Colour Press Ltd

Answers available at www.collins.co.uk/Caribbean

Acknowledgements

The publishers wish to thank the following for permission to reproduce photographs. Every effort has been made to trace copyright holders and to obtain their permission for the use of copyright materials. The publishers will gladly receive any information enabling them to rectify any error or omission at the first opportunity.
(t = top, c = centre, b = bottom, l = left, r = right)

p37l Kakteen/Shutterstock; p37r NOPPHARAT STUDIO 969/Shutterstock

Contents

1 Reading maps

Student's Book pages 4–19

1 Use words from the box to fill in the blank spaces in the sentences below.

Codrington	Caribbean region	108	Antigua	north
sugar	premier	island	Prime Minister	east
St. John's	tourism	south	62	Barbuda	fishing

a The name of the state we live in is called _____ and

_____.

b An _____ is a piece of land completely surrounded by water.

c Our island is part of the _____.

d The Caribbean is _____ of South America,

_____ of North America and _____ of

Central America.

e Antigua is _____ square miles, while Barbuda is

_____ square miles.

f The first _____ was Sir Vere Cornwall Bird.

g The island used to produce _____.

h Today _____ is the main industry of Antigua, while

_____ is the main industry of Barbuda.

i The capital of Antigua is _____, while the capital of

Barbuda is _____.

2 On the map of Antigua, write in the names of the parishes. Use a dot to put in the name and location of a village in each parish.

St. John	New Winthorpes
St. Mary	Liberta
St. Philip	Newfield
St. Paul	Bolans
St. George	Cedar Grove
St. Peter	Parham

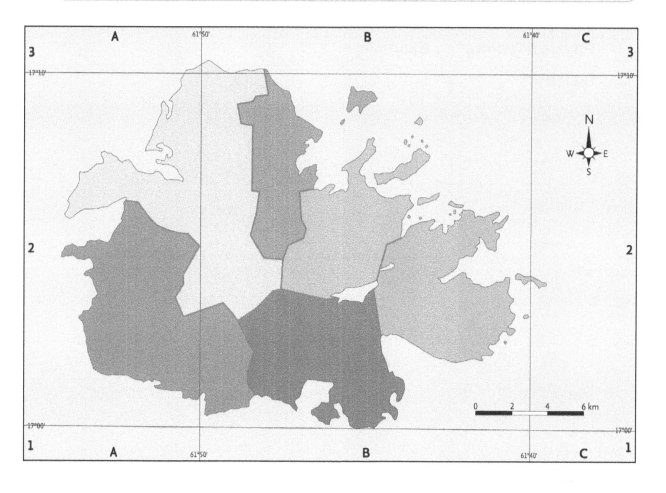

3 Draw a line to match each physical feature on the left to its parish on the right.

a	Christian Cove Swamp	i	St. John
b	Long Bay Beach	ii	St. Mary
c	Mount Obama	iii	St. Philip
d	Bat Cave	iv	St. Paul
e	Paige Pond	v	St. George
f	Wallings Dam	vi	St. Peter

4 Complete the table below with one example in either Antigua or Barbuda of each physical feature.

Physical feature	Example
Beach	
Hill	
Cave	
Dam	
Mangrove swamp	
Pond	
Lagoon	
Rainforest	

5 Mark the physical features you named in Exercise 4 on this map of Antigua. Try to draw a symbol to represent each one.

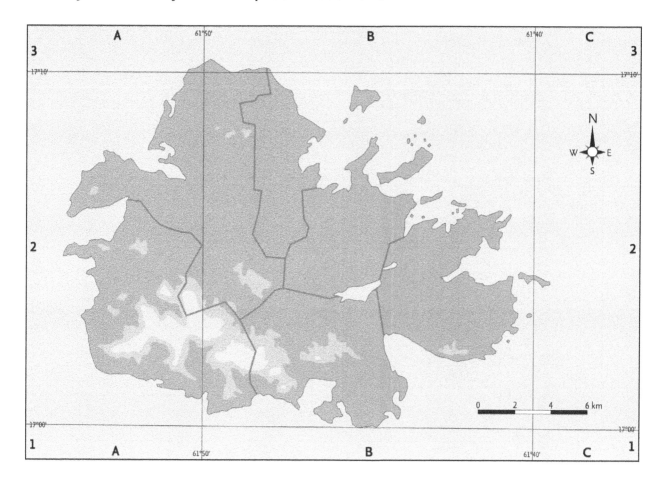

6 Now add these to the map above:

  a create a legend with symbols for a beach, a harbour and a historical site.

  b three examples of each on the map using symbols and the names.

7 Using the cardinal points N, S, E and W, give the directions of the following places on the map.

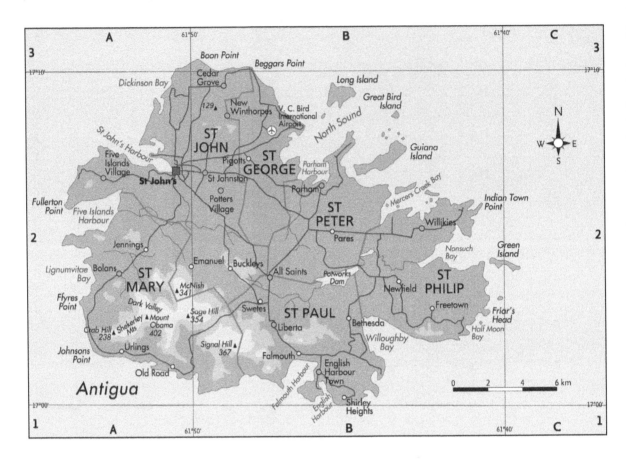

a What is the direction of Bolans from All Saints? _____

b What is the direction of St. John's from Crab Hill? _____

c What is the direction of Falmouth from Parham? _____

d What is the direction of Newfield from All Saints? _____

e What is the direction of Willikies from Freetown? _____

8 Find the words from Unit 1 below in the wordsearch.

R	L	H	W	A	K	U	O	G	E	H	C	F	R	X
J	A	P	I	P	N	J	Q	Q	L	C	O	K	Z	Y
A	C	K	J	L	C	T	U	D	N	A	M	S	P	X
G	I	V	Y	B	L	A	I	A	N	E	P	G	K	W
Y	R	P	Q	M	T	E	E	G	V	B	A	J	H	F
V	O	P	H	O	L	B	L	Z	U	K	S	Y	E	N
B	T	P	R	S	B	C	A	V	E	A	S	X	M	W
M	S	M	H	I	I	Z	P	Y	S	W	V	W	P	L
V	I	C	R	I	B	R	S	M	I	D	O	V	S	P
V	H	A	H	N	J	X	A	V	T	I	B	M	M	S
C	C	H	P	I	N	N	M	P	U	U	W	A	N	E
S	J	M	A	E	N	O	O	G	A	L	W	X	G	T
A	P	U	R	Y	W	B	V	V	Q	S	R	O	G	T
H	V	G	U	S	M	A	N	G	R	O	V	E	K	F
U	W	M	M	T	I	O	K	V	U	J	M	D	E	J

Antigua	beach	Caribbean	cave
compass	Equator	hill	historical
lagoon	mangrove	parish	swamp

9. On the map of Barbuda write the name of one of each of the following, to show where they are on the island: beach, lagoon, Codrington, cave, a high point.

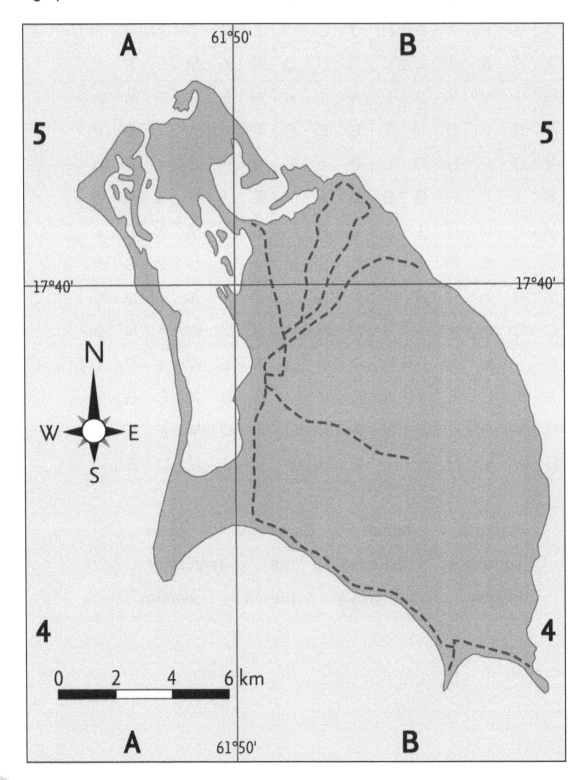

10 On the map of Antigua, use different colours to circle where the following features can be found.

a an airport

b a national park

c a cricket stadium

d a marina

e four points of interest

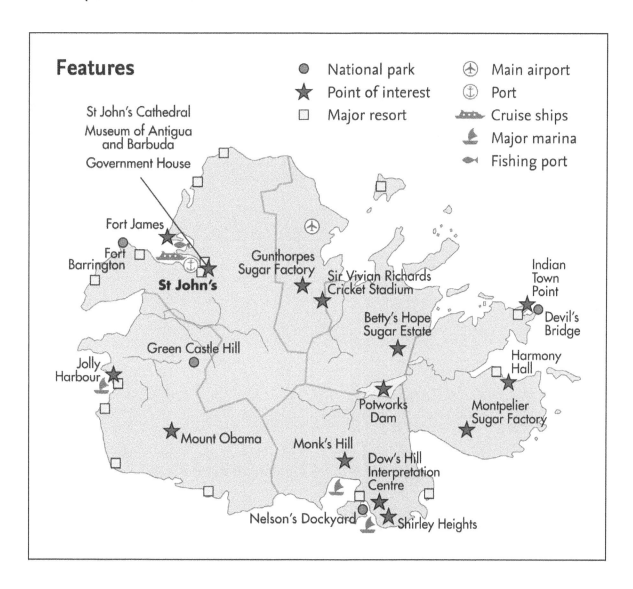

11 On this blank map of the world, draw and label the Equator and write in the Northern and Southern Hemisphere.

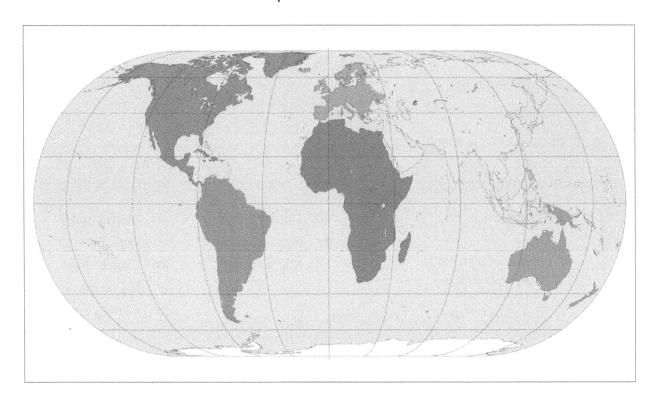

2 Our cultural heritage

Student's Book pages 20–29

1 Use words from the box to fill in the blank spaces in the text below.

Europeans	culture	traditions	music
stories	ancestors	speak	Amerindians
religion	Africans	dance	

The way of life of a group of people is called its _____.

It includes the way we _____, _____, dress,

cook our food, the _____ we play, the _____

we tell and our _____.

The culture we have today came from our _____.

The different groups brought their own cultural _____ when

they came to our islands.

Our national dish, fungee and pepperpot, came from the _____.

Our dialect and dance came from the _____. The language

we speak and major religions came from the _____.

2 On the map of Antigua, colour the areas where the earliest people settled in yellow. Write in the names of the areas.

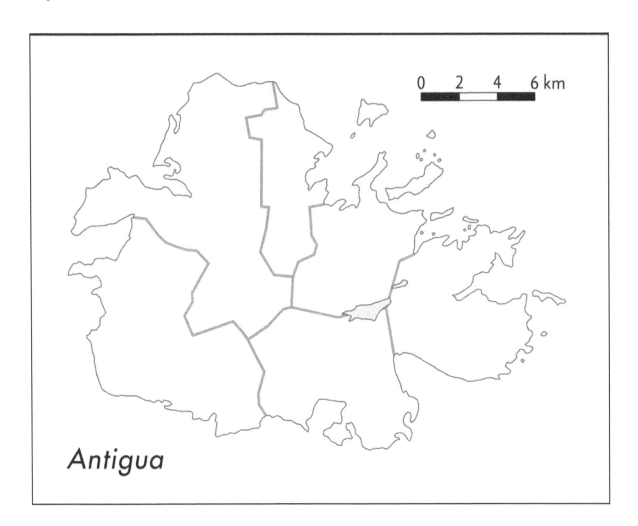

Antigua

0   2   4   6 km

3 Read pages 21–23 in the Student's Book. Complete this ideas map with key information about the Arawaks.

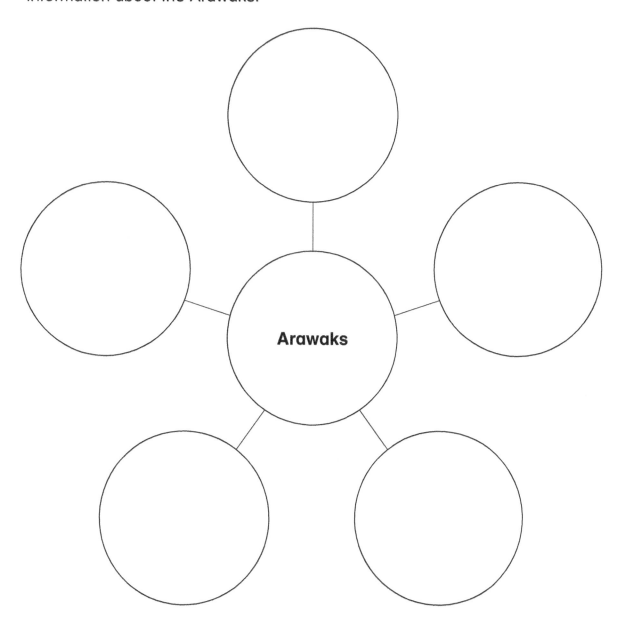

4 Read pages 23–24 in the Student's Book. Complete the ideas map with key information about the Caribs.

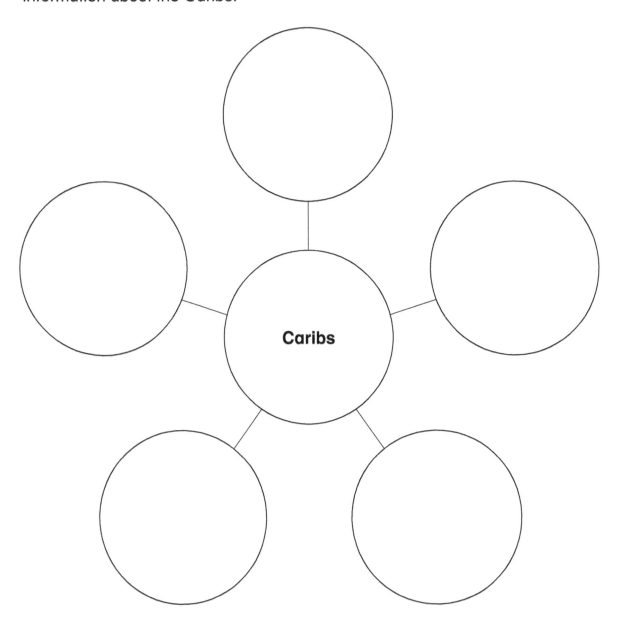

Caribs

5 Use words from the box to fill in the blank spaces in the sentences below.

Dutch	gold	Europeans	Betty's Hope	Spain
British	English Harbour	sugar	1492	
silver	tobacco	Amerindians	Shirley Heights	

a After the Amerindians came the _____.

b Christopher Columbus visited the island in _____.

c He travelled from the country of _____.

d The Spanish came to look for _____ and _____.

e After the Spanish, came the _____, French and

_____.

f They brought crops such as _____ and _____.

g They forced the _____ to work for them.

h They first settled in _____ and used _____ as a look-out point.

i One example of a sugar plantation is _____.

6 Answer the following questions.

a Why did the Africans come to the Caribbean?

_____

b How were they treated?

_____

c When was slavery abolished?

_____

d Why did the Chinese and Indians come to the Caribbean?

_____

e What did they do after their contract was done?

_____

7 In the table below, make a list of all the nationalities in Antigua and Barbuda and write one thing that they are well known for.

Nationality	Known for

8 Read pages 27–29 in the Student's Book and answer the questions.

a

> Joyanna is a new student in your class who doesn't speak English very well.
> When Joyanna is speaking, some of her words don't make sense. Sometimes
> some of the other students laugh at her.

    i   What can you do to help Joyanna?

    _____

    ii   What would you say to your other classmates about their treatment
          of Joyanna?

    _____

    iii   How can we show tolerance to people who may be different from us?

    _____

    _____

b What are some of the local traditions and customs that we have?

_____

_____

c What is Carnival and why do we celebrate it?

_____

_____

d When is Emancipation Day?

_____

e When is Sailing Week?

_____

9 Write the Standard English for the dialect shown in the table.

Dialect	Standard English
cum yah	
nam um	
si dun dey	
put um back	
me head ah hat me	
na nack me	

10 Why is it important to preserve our culture?

_____

_____

11 Draw a line to match each word on the left with its meaning on the right.

a ethnicity		**i**	an early descendant
b ancestor		**ii**	an accepted way of doing something
c culture		**iii**	the passing on of customs
d tradition		**iv**	the way of life of a group of people
e custom		**v**	a group of people living under the same roof
f family		**vi**	a group of people who share the same culture

12 List some of the games that your parents used to play in their younger days.

_____

_____

Find the words from Unit 2 below in the wordsearch.

I	N	P	G	O	G	F	I	D	N	N	E	C	A	D
N	A	T	I	O	N	A	L	I	T	Y	G	U	K	O
D	S	W	R	S	F	W	H	E	N	D	A	S	E	O
T	K	N	Y	A	F	U	R	S	A	M	U	T	H	F
E	C	U	A	A	D	U	L	S	E	Y	G	O	L	A
U	W	H	M	C	T	I	P	P	E	M	N	M	C	C
K	X	I	I	L	I	R	T	O	U	U	A	I	F	S
K	L	O	U	N	E	R	T	I	R	O	L	G	O	I
Y	Y	C	W	S	E	K	F	P	O	X	W	Y	R	V
W	U	B	E	F	I	S	A	A	P	N	S	H	D	O
I	C	R	E	M	Z	J	E	X	E	B	Z	Q	C	L
L	V	R	O	T	S	E	C	N	A	I	D	N	I	O
E	M	U	V	L	I	H	R	F	N	E	K	O	E	V
E	L	D	J	N	Q	Y	U	X	S	X	I	O	E	P
D	I	A	L	E	C	T	U	P	V	M	A	P	F	K

Africans   ancestor   Chinese   culture

custom   dialect   Europeans   family

food   games   Indian   language

nationality   preserve   tradition

3 Government and leaders

Student's Book pages 30–33

1 Use words from the box to fill in the blank spaces in the sentences below.

> pastor   principal   leader   Prime Minister
>
> parent   captain   teacher

a A _____ is someone who directs a group of people.

b The leader of the country is called a _____.

c The leader of a school is called a _____.

d The leader of the class is called a _____.

e The leader of the home is called a _____.

f The leader of the church is called a _____.

g The leader of a sports team is called a _____.

2 What makes a good leader?

_____

_____

_____

_____

3 Make a list of the names of all the leaders you know of in your community.

_____

_____

_____

_____

_____

4 In your own words, explain how a leader is chosen.

_____

_____

_____

_____

5 Say whether you think the following statements are true or false by circling the correct answer.

a A good leader must know how to communicate.   True   False

b A good leader is very dishonest.   True   False

c A good leader steals.   True   False

d A good leader earns respect.   True   False

e A good leader is creative.   True   False

6 In your own words, explain what a government is and give some examples of what it does.

_____

_____

_____

_____

_____

7 How is the government chosen in Antigua and Barbuda?

_____

_____

_____

_____

_____

8 Find the words from Unit 3 below in the wordsearch.

T	T	C	L	A	P	I	C	N	I	R	P	L	R	P
N	N	H	O	E	L	E	A	E	D	E	R	E	O	R
E	O	I	F	N	T	H	L	E	C	O	S	A	T	I
M	C	U	A	N	F	E	T	R	Y	P	I	D	A	M
N	S	H	T	T	C	I	H	E	O	P	R	E	S	E
R	I	M	O	T	P	E	D	N	M	I	N	R	O	M
E	I	S	I	I	T	A	S	E	E	R	J	S	N	I
V	D	O	X	H	C	I	C	A	N	F	Y	N	B	N
O	N	N	F	E	B	E	G	Q	Y	C	L	E	I	I
G	C	E	V	I	T	A	E	R	C	O	E	S	Z	S
A	X	H	L	B	C	M	G	Z	O	N	T	O	X	T
R	U	I	U	I	I	G	R	H	Z	U	Z	H	Y	E
A	T	C	J	R	T	Z	C	K	H	W	P	C	H	R
Y	P	I	A	C	C	S	O	R	H	N	R	S	C	X
G	I	G	N	L	T	H	C	T	T	F	U	S	A	F

captain   choice   chosen   church

confidence   creative   election   government

groups   leader   prime minister   principal

responsibility   school

9 Complete the crossword puzzle using the clues below.

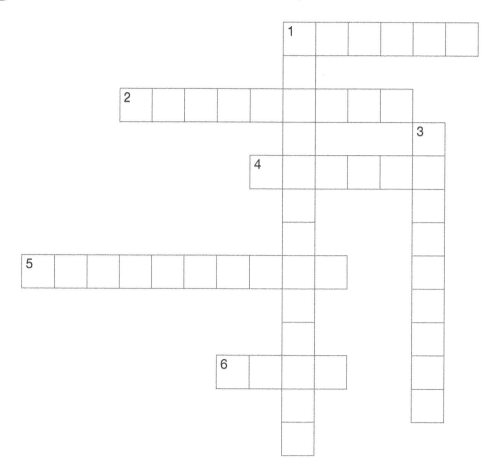

Across

1. Leader of the church

2. How leaders are chosen

4. Someone who guides and directs a group of people

5. A group of people who run the country

6. What people do during elections

Down

1. Leader of the country

3. Leader of the school

4 The natural environment

Student's Book pages 34–45

1 Use words from the box to fill in the blank spaces in the sentences below. Words can be used more than once.

green	landforms	rainfall	climate	physical
blue	dams	hills	maps	water bodies

a _____ give us information on the shape of the land around us.

b Two types of maps are _____ and _____.

c One feature of climate is the amount of _____ that a country gets.

d The natural landscape is made up of _____ and _____.

e Some physical features of Antigua and Barbuda include _____ and _____.

f On a map areas of water are shown in _____ and land at sea level is shown in _____.

g _____ maps tell us about the climate conditions.

h _____ maps tell us about the physical features of a country.

2 Read page 36 in the Student's Book and answer these questions.

a How does the natural landscape affect where and how people live?

_____

_____

_____

b How does the natural landscape affect the climate of a country?

_____

_____

c How does the weather and climate change the natural landscape of a country?

_____

_____

_____

3 Use words from the box to fill in the blank spaces in the text below.

natural disaster	**hurricanes**	**November**
trees	**houses**	**mudslides**

In the Caribbean, _____ are the most common

_____ caused by the weather. They can bring down

_____ and _____ and heavy rains from

flooding can cause _____ and soil erosion. This washes

away the top layers of hills and other high areas of land. Hurricane

season starts at the beginning of June and finishes at the end

of _____ each year.

4 Answer the following questions in your own words.

a Name two effects of a hurricane.

_____

_____

b Name the hurricane that hit Barbuda in 2017.

_____

c What is an earthquake?

_____

_____

d Name two effects of an earthquake.

_____

e Explain the work of two local organisations in taking care of our natural environment in Antigua and Barbuda.

_____

_____

_____

_____

5 Read through the following story about how an earthquake affects a family and answer the questions that follow each section of the story.

It was a normal Saturday evening and the Phillips family was having supper. All of a sudden, their pet dog Lucky started to bark loudly. Then a rumbling sound was heard. Everything around them started shaking violently. The lights went off, the dishes shook, and ornaments were falling from the television stand. Then everyone shouted, "Earthquake!"

a What do you think the family should do?

_____

_____

The shaking came to a stop. They went to look around. The house was a mess, but no one was hurt, including Lucky. Dad warned that there could be some aftershocks.

b What do you think the family should do now?

_____

_____

After a few minutes the electricity went out and they were left in the dark.

c What do you think they should do now?

_____

_____

6 Draw a picture to show what the natural landscape of your community/village looks like.

7 Read pages 40–42 in the Student's Book and answer the questions.

a What is global warming?

_____

_____

_____

b Give two effects of global warming.

_____

_____

c What is deforestation?

_____

_____

d Give two effects of deforestation.

_____

_____

e Name one thing that can be done to prevent deforestation.

_____

_____

f What is dredging?

_____

_____

g Give two effects of dredging.

_____

_____

8 What activity is happening in each of these pictures?

_____   _____

9 Draw a line to match each word or words on the left with its correct meaning on the right.

a physical map

b natural landscape

c climate map

d deforestation

e erosion

f dredging

g pollution

i the clearing of a large area of land

ii shows information about the climate of an area

iii made up of landforms and areas of water

iv shows the physical features of a country

v the dirtying of the environment

vi when soil is washed away by heavy rain

vii removing material from under the sea

10 Find the words from Unit 4 below in the wordsearch.

J	Q	C	P	D	M	U	T	H	Z	E	O	N	W	W
M	I	E	O	H	G	A	B	D	N	B	R	O	S	E
H	G	O	P	A	Y	A	P	V	B	E	G	I	T	A
T	L	L	N	A	A	S	I	N	N	X	A	T	H	T
F	C	N	O	A	C	R	I	A	Z	C	N	U	R	H
V	G	E	Z	B	O	S	C	C	L	Q	I	L	H	E
B	H	S	T	N	A	I	D	I	A	W	S	L	Q	R
K	N	S	M	O	R	L	M	N	Q	L	A	O	W	Y
G	V	E	U	R	R	A	W	I	A	Z	T	P	Y	N
U	N	L	U	V	T	P	E	A	X	L	I	R	B	X
T	R	H	T	E	D	D	Z	G	R	W	O	S	H	L
E	K	A	U	Q	H	T	R	A	E	M	N	W	Z	P
D	R	E	D	G	I	N	G	M	J	F	I	R	E	V
D	E	F	O	R	E	S	T	A	T	I	O	N	K	J
T	H	G	U	O	R	D	Z	O	R	D	A	P	G	M

climate	deforestation	dredging	drought
earthquake	environment	fire	flood
global warming	hurricane	landscape	
lessen	map	organisation	physical
pollution	protect	weather	

5 Our communities

Student's Book pages 46–57

1 Use words from the box to fill in the blank spaces in the sentences below.

access	sparsely	population	10	densely
census	shape			

a _____ is the number of people living in a country at a particular time.

b The count of the population is done through a _____.

c A census is done every _____ years.

d If an area has a lot of people, that area is said to be _____ populated.

e If an area only has a few people, that area is said to be _____ populated.

f There are many reasons why people choose to live in an area. These include the _____ of the land and _____ to transportation.

2 Fill in the diagram to show the factors that affect population density in Antigua and Barbuda.

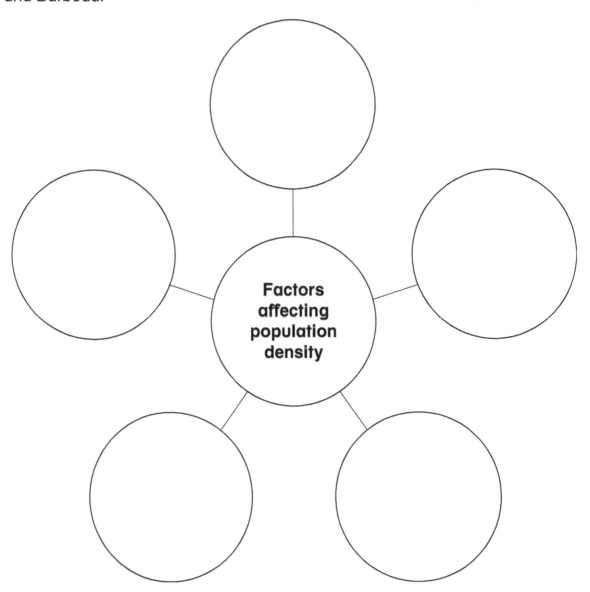

Factors affecting population density

3 Shade the areas on the map of Antigua and Barbuda that are densely populated in green and the areas that are sparsely populated yellow.

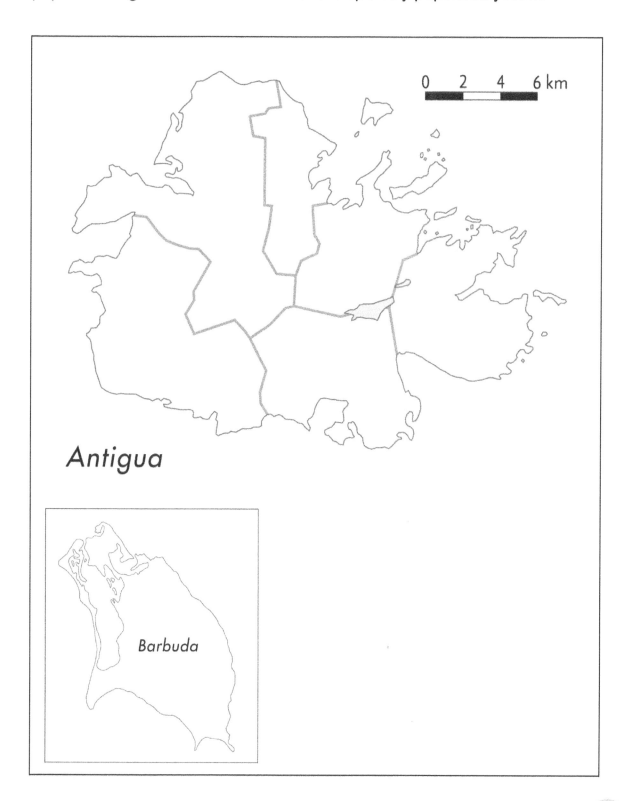

Antigua

Barbuda

0   2   4   6 km

4 Fill in the characteristics of how a settlement usually develops in the diagram below.

Characteristics
of a
settlement

5 In your own words, explain what you think is meant by the following.

a Village

_____

b City

_____

c Town

_____

6 Read pages 49–53 in the Student's Book and answer the questions on communication.

   a What is communication?

      _____

      _____

   b List three ways we used to communicate long ago.

      _____

      _____

   c List four ways we use to communicate today.

      _____

      _____

   d What has caused the changes in the way we communicate, over the years?

      _____

      _____

      _____

   e What is your favourite way to communicate?

      _____

      _____

   f Imagine communication suddenly became very slow again, as it used to be. What problems do you think it might bring?

      _____

      _____

      _____

      _____

7 You are in a competition to design a communication device to be used in the future. Write the name of the device. Draw a picture of it and explain its features (what it can do) in the box.

8 Read pages 54–57 in the Student's Book and answer the questions about transportation.

a What is transportation?

_____

_____

b What are the three forms of transportation?

_____

_____

c What was the only way for people to travel a long time ago, before transportation was invented?

_____

_____

d Name three types of early transportation.

_____

_____

_____

e Name four types of transport used today.

_____

_____

_____

f Explain what is meant by:

i private transport

_____

ii public transportation

_____

g Is there any form of future transportation that you would like to ride in? Why?

_____

_____

_____

h How would you feel if there was no form of transportation available for you to use today?

_____

_____

9 Collect pictures of some different means of transport used in other parts of the world today. Paste them below and add a label to each one to say what it is.

10 Find the words from Unit 5 below in the wordsearch.

N	N	C	L	Y	C	R	A	V	E	W	A	E	N	W
B	O	A	O	R	T	I	R	L	P	T	E	G	O	Q
S	N	I	Z	M	R	I	C	R	N	Y	S	A	I	W
D	H	W	T	P	M	Y	C	E	Q	I	Y	L	T	W
Y	B	A	L	A	C	U	M	N	W	O	T	L	A	S
G	L	A	P	I	T	E	N	G	I	V	N	I	C	P
P	N	E	B	E	L	R	C	I	P	J	Y	V	I	A
E	J	T	S	T	G	P	O	W	T	G	D	C	N	R
E	I	C	T	N	U	L	Q	P	B	Y	Q	G	U	S
N	R	E	C	C	E	N	S	U	S	Z	S	R	M	E
U	S	Z	O	X	X	D	X	T	O	N	D	U	M	L
P	O	P	U	L	A	T	I	O	N	K	A	W	O	Y
Y	T	T	N	O	Y	R	P	N	S	Q	F	R	C	G
V	R	C	T	U	F	W	R	V	T	K	W	F	T	B
H	F	N	N	A	T	W	U	Y	T	I	S	N	E	D

airplane	bicycle	census	city
communication		community	count
densely	density	land	population
sea	settlement	shape	sparsely
town	transportation	village	

48

6 Natural resources

Student's Book pages 58–63

1 Use words from the box to complete the statements below.

> non-renewable   natural   resource
>
> conserving   renewable

a A _____ resource is anything found naturally in the environment.

b _____ is taking care of our resources wisely.

c A _____ is anything that is useful to humans.

d A _____ resource is replaced naturally.

e A _____ resource is not replaced naturally.

2 Make a list in the table of as many natural and man-made resources as you can think of.

Natural resources	Man-made resources

3 Place each of these resources in the table under the correct heading.

sand   water   oil   tree   animals   sunlight

gold   natural gas   plastic   paper   chair

air   rubber

Renewable	Man-made	Non-renewable

4 Read pages 61–62 in the Student's Book and answer these questions about endangered animals.

a What is the meaning of the words 'endangered' and 'extinct'?

endangered: _____

extinct: _____

b Name four animals that are endangered in Antigua and Barbuda.

_____

_____

c Give two reasons why some animals are endangered.

_____

_____

d Say two things that you think can be done to prevent these animals from becoming extinct.

_____

_____

_____

5 Draw a poster showing some ideas for how we can protect our animals from becoming extinct.

6 Answer the questions.

a What is conservation?

_____

_____

b Why do you think it is important for us to conserve our natural resources?

_____

_____

c Give three ways we can conserve our natural resources.

_____

_____

_____

d Imagine that your family often wastes a lot of water at home. What are some of the ways of conserving water that you can share with them?

_____

_____

_____

_____

_____

7 Circle the correct word to finish each of these sentences.

a Resources that are always available are:

renewable

non-renewable

b Resources that can be replaced are:

renewable

non-renewable

c Using our resources wisely means:

reserving them

conserving them

d Resources that must not be used up are:

renewable

non-renewable

e An example of a non-renewable resource is:

oil

trees

f An example of a renewable resource is:

air

diamond

8 Find the words from Unit 6 below in the wordsearch.

S	E	T	T	S	E	C	R	U	O	S	E	R	C	Q
E	G	W	M	G	B	I	R	L	V	L	C	X	E	A
E	C	E	P	U	A	E	A	E	B	U	J	H	N	N
R	C	O	N	S	E	R	V	A	T	I	O	N	D	I
T	X	G	I	V	U	L	W	S	R	A	P	T	A	M
B	V	X	H	T	I	E	O	E	J	R	W	H	N	A
Y	I	D	A	Z	N	R	N	R	O	D	R	G	G	L
L	B	N	I	E	A	E	O	T	T	O	M	I	E	S
F	A	F	R	A	W	N	E	N	D	E	D	L	R	K
S	Q	N	U	A	M	C	H	W	M	F	P	N	E	H
P	O	Z	B	X	T	O	D	E	W	E	N	U	D	A
N	S	L	E	X	T	I	N	C	T	Y	N	S	R	S
R	E	P	P	O	C	M	M	D	Q	G	U	T	Z	A
P	I	U	X	L	T	Y	D	Y	Y	K	X	J	X	K
P	G	I	B	Y	L	J	I	E	Y	N	C	S	H	U

air   animals   conservation   copper

diamond   endangered   environment   extinct

natural   non-renewable   petroleum   protect

renewable   resources   sunlight   trees   water

7 Industries

Student's Book pages 64–68

1 Answer these questions.

a What is an industry?

_____

_____

b List the four types of industries

_____

_____

_____

_____

c In which type of industry do the workers take things from the land and sea?

_____

d In which type of industry is manufacturing used to turn raw materials into something useful?

_____

e In which type of industry is a service provided instead of producing goods?

_____

f In which type of industry do the workers do research?

_____

2 Draw lines to match these workers on the left to the type of industry they work in.

banker

doctor

taxi driver

computer technician   primary

farmer

                                        secondary
basket maker

fisherman

                                        tertiary
teacher

lawyer   quaternary

tailor

carpenter

scientist

3 With the help of your teacher or parents make a list of goods and services that are in the different types of industry. Write them in the table below.

Primary	Secondary	Tertiary	Quaternary

4 For each type of industry listed in the table below, give examples of products that are made and services that are provided. You can use the internet to help you.

Type of industry	Example of goods produced or services provided
fishing	
farming	
cottage	
manufacturing	
agro-processing	
tourism	
banking	

5 If we stopped all primary industry, what do you think would happen to the other types of industry? Give some examples.

_____

_____

_____

_____

6 For each of the raw materials in the table below, list products that they can be made into. Try to find as many as you can. You can use the internet to help.

Raw material	Products
tomatoes	
corn	
mangoes	
wood	
raspberries	

7 Use words from the box to fill in the blank spaces in the text below.

work	food	payment	job	family	salary
bills	tax	country	services	healthcare	
government	wage				

Industries provide _____ for adults to do. This is called a

_____. When adults work, they receive a _____.

This is called a _____ or a _____. The money

earned is used to care for the _____ by doing things such as

buying _____ and paying _____.

Some of the money earned goes to help develop the _____.

This money is called a _____. The tax is collected by the

_____ and used to provide _____ such as

_____ for the people in the country.

8 Draw a line to match each word or phrase on the left with its meaning on the right.

a quaternary industry

b primary industry

c industry

d tertiary industry

e manufacturing

f factory

g secondary industry

i turning raw materials into something useful

ii a building where manufacturing is done

iii any activity that earns money for people

iv taking things from the land and the sea

v taking the things from the land and sea and making them into something useful

vi providing services in exchange for money

vii providing services in the field of research and technology

9 Find the words from Unit 7 below in the wordsearch.

R	A	Y	H	Y	T	E	R	T	I	A	R	Y	P	N
E	Q	L	R	U	R	X	Z	T	V	G	A	R	Q	O
M	M	Q	E	O	V	A	K	R	Y	R	I	P	M	I
R	M	S	I	N	T	Y	N	R	P	M	U	Y	B	T
A	F	R	N	L	T	C	A	R	A	L	R	H	Z	C
F	A	Q	D	B	O	L	A	R	E	A	I	W	R	U
L	F	T	U	T	A	Q	Y	F	D	T	W	N	D	D
M	F	E	S	S	R	M	O	N	E	Y	A	N	K	O
U	H	L	T	O	K	E	O	T	N	L	O	U	Q	R
G	N	I	R	U	T	C	A	F	U	N	A	M	Q	P
H	A	O	Y	V	E	X	P	S	X	W	V	H	L	U
A	M	O	L	S	H	L	B	J	Q	O	P	G	M	O
E	C	I	V	R	E	S	S	E	J	R	K	X	N	P
C	I	J	G	Y	H	V	V	L	F	K	Y	F	M	A
G	E	O	I	V	W	M	A	W	U	U	D	P	P	O

factory   farmer   industry   link

manufacturing   money   primary   production

quaternary   salary   secondary   service

tax   tertiary   work

8 Trade

Student's Book pages 69–73

1 Use words from the box to fill in the blank spaces in the text below.

imported	barter	import	electronics	supply
export	machinery	vehicles	demand	goods
services	trade			

a _____ is the buying and selling of goods and services.

b Exchanging good and services without money is called _____.

c When countries buy goods from another country it is called

_____.

d When countries sell to another country it is called _____.

e Countries trade with each other to get the _____ and

_____ that they need.

f Most of the goods we use are _____ from other countries.

g Examples of goods imported are _____, _____

and _____.

h The quantity of goods produced is called the _____.

i The number of people that need or want a particular product is called

the _____.

2 Answer these questions.

a Why do countries need to trade?

_____

_____

b Explain what is meant by supply and demand.

_____

_____

_____

c What happens to the price of goods when:

i there are more goods than people want or need?

_____

_____

ii there are fewer goods than people want or need?

_____

_____

3 Name some of the products that are imported into Antigua and Barbuda. You can use the internet to help you.

_____

_____

_____

_____

_____

_____

_____

4 Explain how transportation is important in trade.

_____

_____

_____

_____

5 Explain how communication is important in trade.

_____

_____

_____

_____

_____

_____

6 Give an example of how we might use bartering today.

_____

_____

_____

7 With a partner, make up a jingle or song to teach your friends about the importance of trade. Write your song or jingle below.

_____

_____

_____

_____

_____

_____

_____

_____

_____

_____

_____

_____

_____

_____

_____

_____

_____

_____

8 Find the words from Unit 8 below in the wordsearch.

M	D	R	R	C	I	F	L	A	S	T	Z	C	N	O
B	A	P	E	M	T	G	G	O	M	I	J	O	C	I
I	U	T	P	T	J	J	A	L	O	O	I	J	U	X
T	Y	O	E	M	R	X	Q	Y	E	T	Y	V	R	E
R	R	C	Z	R	X	A	X	J	A	N	L	S	R	U
T	D	A	E	C	I	O	B	T	H	O	P	P	E	M
N	Z	F	D	G	L	A	R	Y	L	J	P	Z	N	X
D	A	G	Y	E	Y	O	L	Z	H	C	U	X	C	C
B	L	T	R	O	P	X	E	S	Q	F	S	K	Y	A
W	A	R	U	S	U	K	D	S	C	A	R	C	E	R
J	U	N	N	M	O	N	E	U	S	S	I	V	J	G
W	O	A	X	U	A	X	A	E	H	Q	T	J	R	O
S	R	C	O	M	M	U	N	I	C	A	T	I	O	N
T	C	F	E	Y	M	B	P	N	O	K	G	E	Z	D
O	E	D	S	C	K	S	O	T	J	M	D	G	S	F

barter	cargo	communication	currency
demand	export	import	materials	raw
scarce	ships	supply	trade	transportation

Notes

Notes